What's in this book

学习内容 Contents   2

读一读 Read   4

听听说说 Listen and say   12

写一写 Write   16

多元学习 Connections   18

温习 Checkpoint   20

分享 Sharing   22

T0351543

This book belongs to

_____

多变的天气
The Unpredictable weather

学习内容 Contents

沟通 Communication

说说天气情况
Talk about weather conditions

说说衣着
Talk about clothes

背景介绍：
浩浩一家来到位于美国亚利桑那州，世界著名的自然景观大峡谷（the Grand Canyon）旅行。玲玲和妈妈正在查看大峡谷的地形图，浩浩和爸爸正在查看当地的天气情况。当天天晴，浩浩和爸爸都很开心。

生词 New words

⭐ 天气	weather
⭐ 太阳	sun
⭐ 月亮	moon
⭐ 下雨	to rain
⭐ 下雪	to snow
⭐ 帽子	cap, hat
⭐ 鞋子	shoe
⭐ 太	so
晴天	sunny day
刮风	(of wind) to blow
围巾	scarf
袜子	sock
雨衣	raincoat
雨伞	umbrella
雪人	snowman

Grand Canyon

句式 Sentence patterns

太好了！
It is so good!

太可爱了！
It is so cute!

太冷了！
It is so cold!

跨学科学习 Project

设计一个天气盘，并报道天气
Design a weather plate and report the weather

文化 Cultures

中国不同地区的不同气候
Climates in different parts of China

参考答案：
1　Yes. When my family and I went to the beach last summer, we were caught in a rainstorm./No, I have not.
2　They are reading the map of the Grand Canyon.
3　They are checking the local weather report.

Get ready

1 Have you ever experienced changeable weather during your travels?

2 What are Ling Ling and her mother looking at?

3 What are Hao Hao and his father checking?

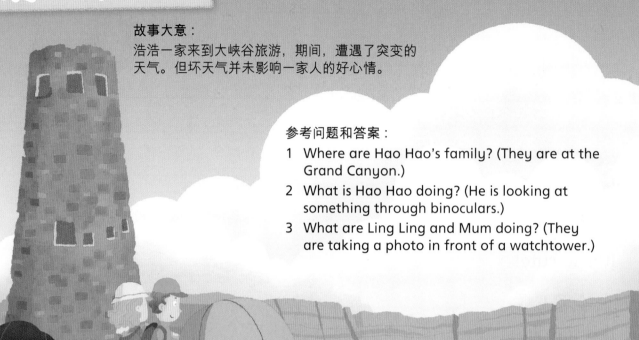

故事大意：

浩浩一家来到大峡谷旅游，期间，遭遇了突变的天气。但坏天气并未影响一家人的好心情。

参考问题和答案：

1　Where are Hao Hao's family? (They are at the Grand Canyon.)

2　What is Hao Hao doing? (He is looking at something through binoculars.)

3　What are Ling Ling and Mum doing? (They are taking a photo in front of a watchtower.)

三月的最后一个星期，我们一家人去大峡谷旅游。

第一天天气很好，太阳和月亮真好看。

晴天
qíng tiān

帽子
mào zi

围巾
wéi jīn

第二天也是晴天，我们戴着帽子和围巾出去了。

参考问题和答案：

1　What is the weather like? (It is sunny and there are white clouds in the blue sky.)

2　What is Ling Ling wearing? (She is wearing a jacket, hat, scarf and gloves.)

路上突然刮风下雨，我们拿出雨衣和雨伞。

参考问题和答案：

1　What is the weather like? (It is raining and the wind is blowing.)
2　What is Ling Ling wearing? (She is wearing a raincoat.)
3　What is Mum holding? (She is holding an umbrella.)

下雪 (xià xuě)

袜子 (wà zi)

鞋子 (xié zi)

然后下雪了，我们的鞋子和袜子都湿了。

参考问题和答案：

1 What is the weather like? (It is snowing.)

2 What happened to Hao Hao's shoes and Ling Ling's socks? (They are wet.)

参考问题和答案：

1 Does the bad weather upset Hao Hao and Ling Ling? (No, they look happy.)
2 What do Hao Hao and Ling Ling want to do? (They want to make a snowman.)

但是我们很高兴。"太好了！下吧，下吧！我们要堆雪人！"

Let's think

1 Recall the story and number the pictures. Write in Chinese.

四

五

三

二

一

2 Design funny weather signs to show the weather in the photos. Ask your friend to talk about the photos and match the signs to them.

这里真热！
人真多。

这里很冷。
天很黑。

左右下角的图文分别匹配图一和图四，学生可参考这两个例子来设计创意天气图标。
图二参考表达：今天下雨。雨真大。图三参考表达：今天刮风。

New words

延伸活动：
学生两人一组玩猜图游戏。每次一人选择一张图片描述，另一人根据描述猜猜说的是哪张图片。描述的学生尽量使用每张图上的所有生词。

1 Learn the new words.

天气　下雨　雨伞　雨衣

现在下雨，天气不好。
玲玲有雨伞，浩浩有雨衣。

太阳　晴天　太好了！　袜子　鞋子

今天有太阳，是晴天。爸爸和浩浩的衣服、裤子、鞋子和袜子很好看。爸爸说："太好了！"

月亮　刮风

现在刮风。黄色的月亮圆圆的，真好看！

下雪　帽子　围巾　雪人

今天下雪。看，雪人！它有帽子和围巾。

2 Listen to your teacher and point to the correct words above.

听听说说 Listen and say

 1 Listen carefully. Circle the mistakes.

2 Look at the pictures. Listen to the story a

昨天刮风下雨，今天早上下雪，现在有太阳了。

 天气太冷了，我的帽子和围巾给它。

 还有"鞋子"！

1 In Picture 3, why is Ling Ling putting her hat and scarf on the snowman? (Because she thinks it is too cold outside.)

2 Have you built a snowman before? (Yes, I have./ No, I have not.)

 这个雪人太可爱了！

 他的肚子比我的大。

你们看，月亮出来了，别玩了。

 雪人雪人，明天见。

3 **Look and role-play with your friend.** 提醒学生从下往上完成题目，参考表达见下。

今天是……
太好了！

今天是晴天。太好了！

刮风了。我的帽子在哪里？

……了。……
在哪里？

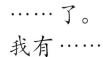

……了。
我有……

下雨了。我有雨衣。

今天下雪。天
气太……我戴
着……

今天下雪。天气太冷了。
我戴着帽子和围巾。

 13

Task

Draw yourself in your favourite and least favourite weather conditions and discuss with your friend.

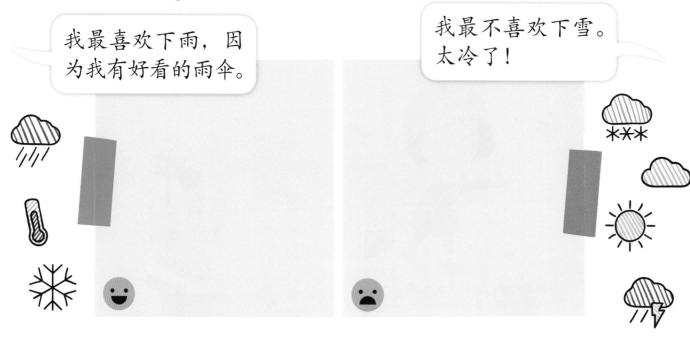

Game 开始游戏前先给学生一些时间浏览一遍本题的图片和文字。

Work with your friend and listen to your teacher. One of you point to the correct word group. The other point to the corresponding picture. See who is faster.

Chant

🎧 05 Listen and say.

天气，天气，
可爱的天气。

白天有太阳，
晚上有月亮。

天气，天气，
多变的天气。

一会儿下雨，
一会儿天晴。

一会儿下雪，
一会儿刮风。

你拿雨伞和雨衣，
我拿围巾上学去。

朗读儿歌前先让学生标注重点词：圈出与天气有关的词语（太阳、月亮、下雨、天晴、下雪、刮风）、用方框框出一个雨具（雨伞）、用下划线划出与衣物有关的词语（雨衣、围巾）。然后学生三人一组，每人选三个词语，各自在三张纸上画出对应的图。朗读时当说到自己选中的词语时马上举起对应图片，看看是否全班同学都能举对图片。

生活用语 Daily expressions

天气真好。
The weather is great.

天气不太好。
The weather is not very good.

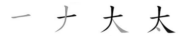

写一写 Write

1 Trace and write the characters.

提醒学生，"太"字的一点不能穿出一撇，"雨"字内部的四点不能写成短横。

一 ナ 大 太

太阳	太阳
太阳	

一 厂 厅 币 币 雨 雨 雨

雨	雨	雨	雨

2 Write and say.

太阳 圆圆的，真好看。

下雨了。雨真大。

3 Fill in the blanks with the correct words. Colour the stars using the same colours.

绿色
下雨

黄色
我

粉色
因为

蓝色
太阳

这是 我 的狗。它喜欢晴天，因为 它爱去外面玩。今天天气很好，有 太阳 ，没有 下雨 。我 和它在花园里玩球。

拼音输入法 Pinyin input

1 Listen to your teacher and compete with your friend. Who can finish typing the words on the sweets of the same colour faster?

yáng	fàn	xuě	mào	xiào	wán
阳	饭	雪	帽	笑	玩
jīn	yuè	zǐ	pàng	qì	è
今	月	子	胖	气	饿
yuán	lèi	tài	chī	zǎo	xié
圆	累	太	吃	早	鞋
tiān	huà	liàng	yún	yǔ	jiā
天	画	亮	云	雨	家

红色的糖果。开始！

2 Challenge yourself. Can you type all of the words above in two minutes?

Cultures

哈尔滨别名"冰城"，冬长夏短，最有名的是冰雕。北京四季分明，虽然秋天很短暂，但秋高气爽，是一年旅游的最佳季节。昆明四季如春，鲜花常开，所以又称"春城"。三亚被称为"中国夏威夷"，有美丽的海滨风光。

The climate in China varies across the country because of its size. Can you match the descriptions to the photos? Write the letters and talk about the weather of each city. 告诉学生，根据方向图标提示，哈尔滨在最北边，三亚在最南边。提醒他们根据城市指示牌的方向将城市与照片配对，再将照片比对文字，确定答案。

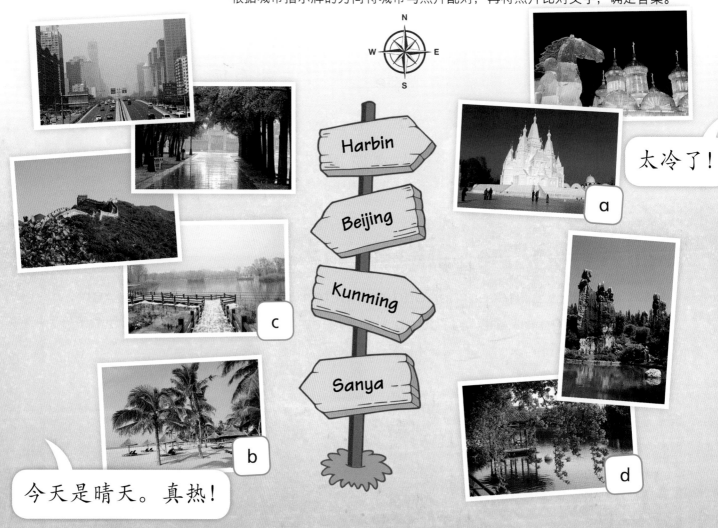

a

It has the coldest and longest winter among China's major cities.

b

It has a tropical climate and never snows during winter. There are typhoons in the summer.

c

It has four distinct seasons: a dry and windy spring, a hot and rainy summer, a cool and brief autumn and a cold winter.

d

It has a very mild climate. It is known as 'the City of Eternal Spring'.

第二题制作材料：一个小号纸盘、一个中号纸盘、一个大号纸盘、彩色笔、一个纸制指针、一个扣针。

1 What is the weather like this week in your city? Watch the weather report and draw the weather signs.

星期……	日	一	二	三	四	五	六	日
天气	☀							

2 Work with your friends. Make a weather plate and report the weather of this week.

将中号纸盘分成六等分，涂色区分，再在每个扇形区域边缘画一件衣物或雨具。

将大号纸盘分成七等分，涂色区分，再在每个扇形区域边缘写上一星期的七天。

①  ② 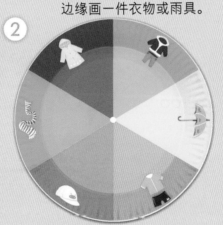 ③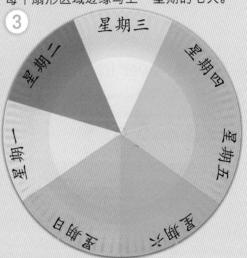

将小号纸盘分成五等分，涂色区分，再在每个扇形区域上画一种天气。

① + ② + ③ + ④ ↓ + ⑤

将三个纸盘从小到大叠加在一起，指针的末端置于纸盘中心，再用扣针穿过纸盘中心并扣好。

太好了！星期日是晴天，有太阳。请戴帽子，别穿太多衣服。

星期一……

延伸活动：
两人一组，一人将转动转盘，另一人根据指针所指的天气、衣物和日期作天气报告。

游戏方法：
学生从 Start 开始，依次回答雪人的问题，回答正确即可获得问题对应的奖牌。到达终点时，将自己获得的奖牌数目与下方的奖杯列表对比，看看自己能拿到哪座奖杯。

1 Answer the snowmen's questions correctly to collect the medals. Which trophy can you get?

这是什么？
Answer in Chinese.

这是月亮。

这是下雨还是下雪？
Answer in Chinese.

下雪。

Start

Complete the sentence and read it aloud.

你喜欢运动吗？你累不累？ Answer in Chinese.

我喜欢/
不喜欢运动。
我累/不累。

中文怎么说？

My shoes are too small.

我的鞋子太小了。

今天天气太冷了。看，我有……和帽子。

围巾

你会看、会说吗？

昨天刮风。
今天是晴天。

Write the character.

我有 雨 伞。

今天天气好吗？

今天有 太阳，
太热了。

Finish

1–2 : 　　3–5 : 　　6–7 : 　　8 :

评核方法：
学生两人一组，互相考察评价表内单词和句子的听说读写。交际沟通部分由老师朗读要求，学生再互相对话。
如果达到了某项技能要求，则用色笔将星星或小辣椒涂色。

2 Work with your friend. Colour the stars and the chillies.

Words	说	读	写
天气	☆	☆	🌶
太阳	☆	☆	☆
月亮	☆	☆	🌶
下雨	☆	☆	☆
下雪	☆	☆	🌶
帽子	☆	☆	🌶
鞋子	☆	☆	🌶
太	☆	☆	☆
晴天	☆	🌶	🌶

Words and sentences	说	读	写
刮风	☆	🌶	🌶
围巾	☆	🌶	🌶
袜子	☆	🌶	🌶
雨衣	☆	☆	☆
雨伞	☆	🌶	🌶
雪人	☆	🌶	🌶
太好了!	☆	🌶	🌶
太可爱了!	☆	🌶	🌶
太冷了!	☆	🌶	🌶

Talk about weather conditions	☆
Talk about clothes	☆

3 What does your teacher say?

My teacher says ...

评核建议：
根据学生课堂表现，分别给予"太棒了！
(Excellent!)"、"不错！(Good!)"或"继续努力！
(Work harder!)"的评价，再让学生圈出上方对
应的表情，以记录自己的学习情况。

分享 Sharing

Words I remember

天气	tiān qì	weather
太阳	tài yáng	sun
月亮	yuè liang	moon
下雨	xià yǔ	to rain
下雪	xià xuě	to snow
帽子	mào zi	cap, hat
鞋子	xié zi	shoe
太	tài	so
晴天	qíng tiān	sunny day
刮风	guā fēng	(of wind) to blow
围巾	wéi jīn	scarf
袜子	wà zi	sock
雨衣	yǔ yī	raincoat
雨伞	yǔ sǎn	umbrella
雪人	xuě rén	snowman

Other words

大峡谷	dà xiá gǔ	the Grand Canyon
旅游	lǚ yóu	to travel
戴	dài	to wear
出去	chū qù	to go out
突然	tū rán	suddenly
拿出	ná chū	to take out
然后	rán hòu	then
湿	shī	wet
但是	dàn shì	but
下	xià	to fall
要	yào	to want to
堆	duī	to build

延伸活动：
1 学生用手遮盖英文，读中文单词，并思考单词意思；
2 学生用手遮盖中文单词，看着英文说出对应的中文单词；
3 学生两人一组，尽量运用中文单词分角色复述故事。

OXFORD
UNIVERSITY PRESS

Oxford University Press is a department of the University of Oxford.
It furthers the University's objective of excellence in research, scholarship,
and education by publishing worldwide. Oxford is a registered trade mark of
Oxford University Press in the UK and in certain other countries

Published in Hong Kong by
Oxford University Press (China) Limited
39th Floor, One Kowloon, 1 Wang Yuen Street, Kowloon Bay,
Hong Kong

Illustrated by Anne Lee, KK Ng and Wildman

Photographs for reproduction permitted by Dreamstime.com

China National Publications Import & Export (Group) Corporation is an authorized distributor of
Oxford Elementary Chinese.

Please contact content@cnpiec.com.cn or 86-10-65856782

ISBN: 9978-0-19-082253-8

10 9 8 7 6 5 4 3 2

Teacher's Edition
ISBN: 978-0-19-082265-1

10 9 8 7 6 5 4 3 2